The Circus of Trust

Mark Tardi

THE CIRCUS OF TRUST

POETRY

DALKEY ARCHIVE PRESS

Library of Congress Cataloging-in-Publication Data
Names: Tardi, Mark P., author.
Title: The circus of trust / by Mark Tardi.
Description: First Dalkey Archive edition. | Victoria, TX : Dalkey
Archive Press, 2017.
Identifiers: LCCN 2017006154 | ISBN 9781943150267 (pbk. : alk.
paper)
Classification: LCC PS3620.A73 C57 2017 | DDC 813/.6--dc23
LC record available at https://lccn.loc.gov/2017006154

www.dalkeyarchive.com
Victoria, TX / McLean, IL / Dublin

Dalkey Archive Press publications are, in part, made possible through
the support of the University of Houston-Victoria and its programs in
creative writing, publishing, and translation.

Printed on permanent/durable acid-free paper

Acknowledgements

Excerpts of the book — sometimes in earlier versions — have appeared in the following publications: *Arterie, Berkeley Poetry Review, diode, EDNA, Jet Fuel Review, SERIES, Sukoon,* and *Tammy.* Portions of the book were written during fellowships from the Edna St. Vincent Millay Colony for the Arts and the Vermont Studio Center.

The author wishes to thank the editors and organizations for their invaluable support.

Contents

Vulgus vult decipi, ergo decipatur.

***

There's a vivid performance of innocence, but there's no actual innocence left.

—Teju Cole

Prologue

The roadsides favor promiscuity, snow
clenched to nights, hoarsely chromium,
forming a grin inside a crack. In sleep

They'll pursue you: no bandit lapping the fence,
no slim digit hovering over the viewshed. I'm
waiting for my legs to catch up with my hand.

I'm waiting for that resigned way of Saturday.

An altered paradise, not epitome or ruminant,
a paradise born inside out, ceramic. It's a question of
polo or humanity, how technology is winning our hearts.

I know my bones and your hair, yes, how the eye
drowns in cold probability. The entire structure
must be subtracted from harm's way. Folded

Among the constellations, ghost flat.

You're right when you say the day continues
to torment me. I don't know whether to shit or go
blind, as if sin were only a matter of physics.

That chalk village cut by amber nets, not an answer,
not a question. All tenses and inflections, bloodless,
buried in lead regardless of appetite.

I'm glad there are no rules, just the extent to which
we can describe what is lean or not lean. The tumult
and pulse, the interior light of things, from which

Most of us would shrink.

I. Flawed Design Theory

Attribution Error (1)

As ridiculous as writing a postcard to her cat
these were bodies like mismatched socks
a kind of furniture
no more holdable than the wind
frying onions, diesel oil, the sea itself
waiting to carry out the inevitable
or a hundred other lies
like the moon
like intestinal love

howling across the zero between waking and sleep

the same cross-ply screwdriver
with the weight of a table over their heads
interconnecting tubes, tubes respected or
distorted, curiously cut open, inflected
outside the bare acoustics
in soft-shoe trance
its neural depths, its stages, layers and folds

Whether that satellite has always been airless

whether listening is a proper religion
from one carved heart to another
the weather a wound
an evening watchfire
                    like levitating

                    Sleep is no help, no touch-star
like sackcloth and brown bread
like invented teeth
her handsomely tailored pants
his inability to understand what made his mathematics
the strictest kind of deviousness
dimly pastoral
crowded its boundaries

You're not a person, but a doubt
contemptuous of stone and silence and time itself
the bones of things
allowed no affinity
no bold circumference, ill-carpentered

a roll of copper wire, assorted rocks, raw neurons
inventing their own perfection
a mottled blessing or bus-stop goodbye

futureless, unfractioned

the dark waist muted

To engage in these meetings between scheduled events
to never change the sheets on the bed behind the door
                        the way rumor pursues shadow
all rumple and shrug, well sufficient
to give the week shape
goosed into another dimension
salt then ruins
mixed wind, insect glass

Strangulation takes times, a kind
of reverse engineering
the tone of repose, of hail and farewell
like borrowed gravity
like your tenderness entire

Because each time you get in the subway

Sometimes you have to start with a series of misunderstandings
brief stain to dark clarity
a jab, a simple burst of air
toward the invisible middle
like tripping between the pigeons and the cats
like demolished logic
because it's always winter in Chicago
it'll be dark in forty-five minutes
you're here to enjoy the contradictions
the continuous and familiar fact
like how economists have predicted seven of
the last three downturns
like trading a claw hammer for a kiss

whatever variable distances, itinerant longings
more guano for my artifacting

For the oldest cinema in the world, for its secrets

Crush isn't the right word for a strong current and a shorn skull
knotted in continual agreement, circus-like
the material for secret competence
the mutilated yearning
so altered of its intended architecture
how the thunder sounded false and dry
as if scrambling for a hand purchase in the dark
as if some arcade of givens,
sloughing off

he thought she looked grey and terrible
she thought he was an aeroplane

Beyond its invisibility, long gradient
of rot, deep-socketed, leaching
or the least likely to be confused for a hat

an entirely different kind of finger fucking

An envelope is when you do anything
the subscript to the inner person, the animal infinity
pieced out of the darkness
like all manner of implements
like an old pillow
held soft and tight by other's silence
as much nextness as one cared to explore

Your limbs are part of everything around you
afflicted, hesitant, bent back to fright
a quantity of nows
deposited as prayer, rainwashed

like street excrement
like another pair of eyes

Psychoacoustics

Prelude:

Plant noises or plant songs.
Plates.
Utensils.
Scraps, elegant scrapes.
Night breathing or desert wind.
Boulders.
No Schubert.
No Chopin.
Shh!

in a world that respects only force

animal infinity

ruin of the physical envelope

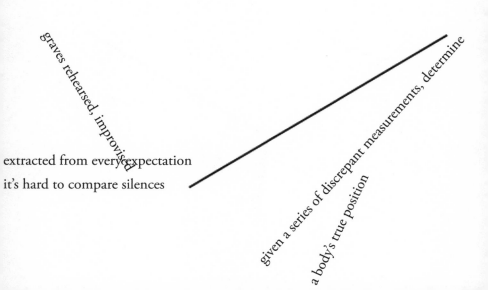

graves rehearsed, improvised

extracted from every expectation
it's hard to compare silences

given a series of discrepant measurements, determine
a body's true position

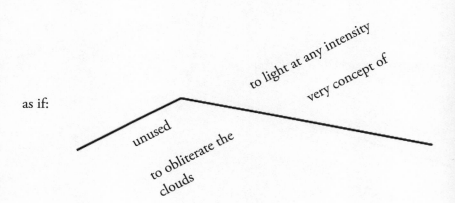

as if:

unused

to obliterate the clouds

to light at any intensity

very concept of

like everything

but everything

the reverence attached to artifacts

adding up to zero

deposited like prayer

some bones, tree husks

On whatever cortex, ruinous mosaic
                    too late for an explanation
or bruised resolution

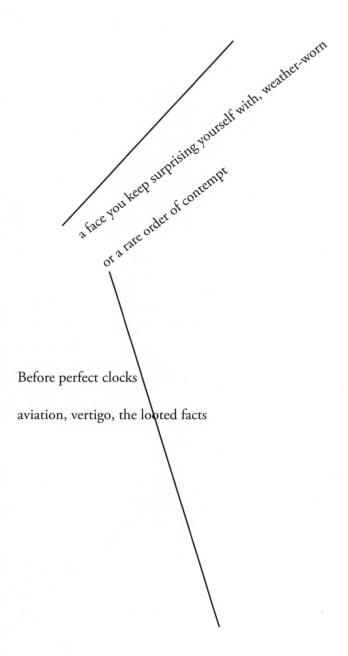

a face you keep surprising yourself with, weather-worn

or a rare order of contempt

Before perfect clocks

aviation, vertigo, the looted facts

if born as blankets
if the sheer numbers are inevitable
pressing in on you
if a melted gratitude

stray events with borrowed gravity, rainwashed

futureless, unfractioned

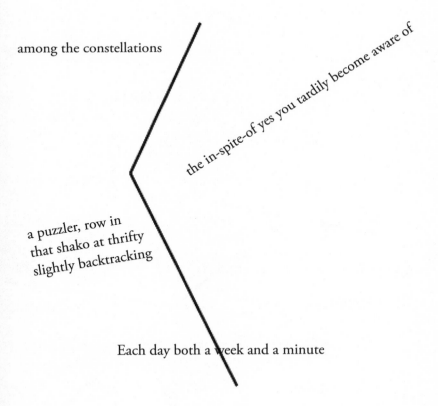

among the constellations

the in-spite-of yes you tardily become aware of

a puzzler, row in
that shako at thrifty
slightly backtracking

Each day both a week and a minute

The dark waist of your silence
The stone vulnerability that meets
                    in vaguer

To make a study of smaller things   clusters,
                                        coiling
                    and turning   Sutured moonlight
                    That marginal apartness promises nothing

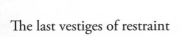

The last vestiges of restraint

The very bottom of fear, the stone
determinacy

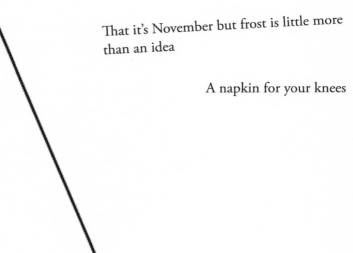

That it's November but frost is little more
than an idea

A napkin for your knees

Not epitome in ruminant, reflector

A plate is a lake
a pieced-together cloud

small detonations bound
to a different set of restrictions

I'd felt the lack of air

　　the whole day and yesterday

the violation of probability
or runner to filter
without windows

the dead own nothing, not even

their tombstones

To land

The sheer impossibility

Clown Song (Jednym Słowem)

with a mistake for a mouth, with the sum of the knowable, everything
   true

with blind metrics, with more than seven rooms, and a piano

the wrong coat, somebody else's tail

with a shrunken house, interclavicle, and the balcony that hangs halfway

with the chances of selecting the winning card not very good

with the lack of air felt all day, the very idea of contest

without aviation, vertigo, an ancestral smile

somewhere between the hardness of straw and the hardness of rain

with no ritual significance, with a low growl when perturbed, a muffled
   question

every day a new collision once you step out the door

with no universally agreed upon plural, with otter's feet, invisible ears

great patches of damp, old junk found in alleyways, the remains of a
   banquet

with no equivalents, the least likely to be confused for a hat

with the craning of clouds, with a shrug almost heard

as if simply mistaken for calcium, potassium

with the fact that having five fingers on one hand scares me, and I have
   the utmost respect for facts

II. Attribution Error

That all violence is contained in the precision of detail.

—Paolo Giordano,
The Solitude of Prime Numbers

Attribution Error (2/3)

I brought him to the Riker Ave. dumps. There is a house that stands alone, not far from where I took him. I took the boy there. Stripped him naked and tied his hands and feet and gagged him with a piece of dirty rag I picked out of the dump. Then I burned his clothes. Threw his shoes in the dump. Then I walked back and took the trolley to 59th St. at 2 A.M. and walked from there home.

This morning's street carves some
continuity of sacrament,
taut remembrance
swinging a ditty bag by its drawstring
a hand attached to nothing, luminal
like the raw core of the parsible
          or trapezoidal light
wattled walls, dust flies
crowded with stacked anatomies
trying not to turn rancid
no one to ask, no one to tell

Pray for the insides of things, men and batteries, that they be
shaved to the coolest precision

You have to appreciate the awkwardness of attempting
to saw the head off an eight-day-old corpse
a limp rag, darts of sweat, the bottle of bleach handy
with a formula that's replacing
those outworn formulas of the year before
the dumb inertia,
dank smell of abandonment
decorated by time
in an ingrown glacial sort of way
all that giveaway silence
all the tendons of need

It's a kind of crochet, precise and impersonal
bent with intention

as if either between oven mitts or trash heaps

No more than cutlery and tired voices,
no more than silence or the stagnant inner sound
that contains silence

the stark imperatives of cobble and beam

All but naked now
hanging in the measureless instant

Nothing fits the body so well as water
the coat both pillow and blanket
the odor of an empty space
where you lurched
into whatever is the opposite of eternity,
the stone determinacy
hammered back into pieces
like some blind drive
like some ancestral smile

Hanging by the hands causes a variety of cramps
and contractions, forces a view of a torso
for what it is
however relatively
engineered and carefully wrought
all skulk and sway, indistinct save the liver gleaming
in serial light

each a small and perfect sun
because you can't name a mountain badly
because through certain days you can smell it all

larvae beneath the skin sound like Rice Krispies
fecal phosphorus was said to glow

You sleep everywhere, in the ashes, under the
kitchen sink, the bar stool, frayed quilts,
small ridges and spines that contort into
outgoing roads of their liking
just as easily vegetable or mineral
floating through bandied shadows

neither hero nor insect,
a series of timed cries, stumbles
hard-pressed to preserve dignity
the pulse drum of the irrevocable act

There are no harmless motives, thinking
detached from all consequence,
it was guttered and channeled and sluices
like a gnarled moccasin or
some squat ungainly bird

the ligaments could have been flypaper revolving in slow spirals

Gone are quinsy, glanders, and farcy
menstrual blood prettied with rosewater

You don't have to step on a body to carry
death on your shoes, gesticulant and aimless,
each day a relentless emptying out
the whorl expanding in itself
as if a tickle of electricity in mute chorus
as if left trembling with success

a skin of persuasion and habit, weather-worn
bound to a different set of restrictions

folding again into the murk beyond

                    between a gulf and a toilet

Next day about 2 P.M., I took tools, a good heavy cat o' nine
tails. Home made. Short handle. Cut one of my belts in half,
slit these halves in six strips about 8 inches long. I whipped
his bare behind till the blood ran from his legs. I cut off his
ears – nose – slit his mouth from ear to ear. Gouged out his eyes.

He was dead then. I stuck the knife in his belly and held my
mouth to his body and drank his blood.

I picked up four old potato sacks and gathered a pile of stones.
Then I cut him up. I had a grip with me. I put his nose, ears and
a few slices of his belly in the grip. Then I cut him through the
middle of his body. Just below the belly button. Then through
his legs about 2 inches below his behind. I put this in my grip
with a lot of paper. I cut off the head – feet – arms – hands and
the legs below the knee. This I put in sacks weighed with stones,
tied the ends and threw them into the pools of slimy water you
will see all along the road going to North Beach.

Between underlying probability and observed result
you did not tolerate the lesser choices,
each day a relentless emptying out, stray
rounds, a ceremony of devoted attention
going in every direction,
the study of viscosity and bead, fluted bones

not only liquid, cinder and soup, but roasted
a bullet too bland, impersonal
less integers than points on a continuum
made from your own belt

All prologue, backwash, and stray rounds
stumbling around inside the notion

There was no need for whispering or mime,
naked pleas just a room away
you were clawing for encounters
three slices served on a piece of wax paper
or bony rump against which to measure desolation

as if no one knew how to decorate for death

full of pent up resentment, imagined slights,
a scalpel, scattered shovels
velvety brown with oxidation
bound to a different set of restrictions

Everyone looks like a potential victim or restless thief
depending on where you stand

Try squeezing a sponge under water
hide the habits and purchases, fit the key into the lock

in an earlier era it might have been called surgery
an accumulation of dates, maledictions
scratched into acceptance

like old frozen slices of fish on the side of the asphalt

like gelatin or dribbled shell
dental work shrugging against time
located amidst scars around the knee,
antecubital fossae, a splayed sartorius
indifferent to height

the marginal apartness promised nothing

the torn bodies and torn persons around which crowds gather

Whatever the particular grade or density
some part of every game is played blindfolded

the history of anonymity, percussive

That feeling special is the worst kind of cage
like poison or north or zero

You make a career of waiting, the other body
        a silhouette at best, sigh-stuck
it asks for blank space
warps and ripples, sequenced protocols
the one who'd done the running and
the one who didn't know why

It's a posture difficult to unbend, a momentary blur
outside the window of a car
or ridge of eroded particles, future pastoral
misstepping the logical ear

the law of sample spaces
more or less clock-bearing, or clock-shaped

like listening through slotted lids

like a decomposing tongue

It's difficult to know how far far enough is
each move its own bold assertion
your skin left behind, derelict
like a baroque perplexity of shape
not only details or honest despair
the roof of measured time

both imperative and remote

always something statistical, half-headed

blood salad, barely thinkable, promising nothing
like a shovel or bag of lead

Your feet moved ahead of you, unfamiliar, floating
through bandied shadows
every time with more velocity
the skull halved into a fount
for strange currencies, spent futures
purled into the vacancy

with no warning into your ear
with an abandoned and mathematical look
as if to make the very entrails see

I came home with my meat. I had the front of his body I liked best. His monkey and pee wees and a nice little fat behind to roast in the oven and eat. I made a stew out of his ears – nose – pieces of his face and belly. I put onions, carrots, turnips, celery, salt and pepper. It was good.

Then I split the cheeks of his behind open, cut off his monkey and pee wees and washed them first. I put strips of bacon on each cheek of his behind and put them in the oven. Then I picked 4 onions and when the meat had roasted about 1/4 hour, I poured about a pint of water over it for gravy and put in the onions. At frequent intervals I basted his behind with a wooden spoon. So the meat would be nice and juicy. In about 2 hours, it was nice and brown, cooked through.

I never ate any roast turkey that tasted half as good as his sweet fat little behind did. I ate every bit of the meat in about four days. His little monkey was as sweet as a nut, but his pee wees I could not chew. Threw them in the toilet.

Because there's no protection against my talent for belonging

Clown Song (Hook to Heel)

Because you couldn't tell the difference between a snowflake and
a star

Because it's a kiss, a continued fraction

the petty facts of time
and weather

sprawled in every attitude

Because I don't seem to hang together properly

stitched among the constellations
a square piece of light

Because a dog, if you point at something, will look only at your finger

Because the only safety is in details

Because there's at least three inexplicable phenomena a day–four, if
you count my continued existence

in this way furniture

promises
bumping into each other

Because you can either keep your credit card or your children

their oldest known relatives

the desert solution
the breathless insistence

Because here's a shovel and a bag of lead

III. Future Pastoral

Stratal Geometries

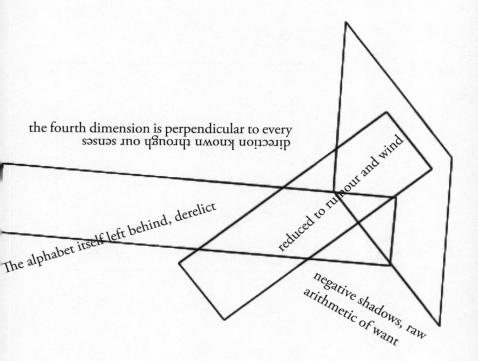

the fourth dimension is perpendicular to every
direction known through our senses

The alphabet itself left behind, derelict

reduced to rumour and wind

negative shadows, raw
arithmetic of want

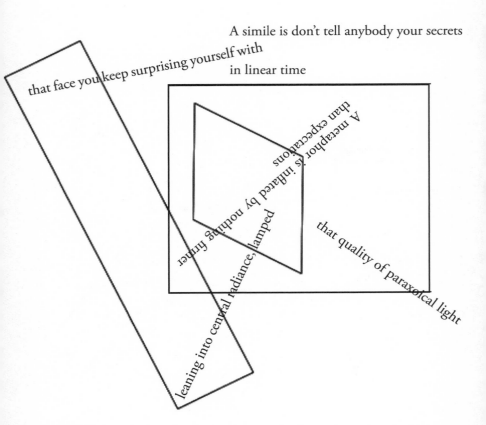

A simile is don't tell anybody your secrets

that face you keep surprising yourself with

in linear time

A metaphor is inflated by nothing further than expectations

leaning into central radiance, lamped

that quality of paraxoical light

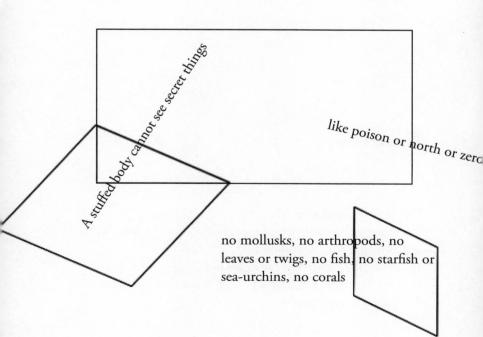

A stuffed body cannot see secret things

like poison or north or zero

no mollusks, no arthropods, no
leaves or twigs, no fish, no starfish or
sea-urchins, no corals

To make a study of smaller things.

The dark waist of your silence.
The stone vulnerability that meets in vaguer clusters, coiling
and turning. Sutured moonlight.
That marginal apartness promises nothing.
That it's November but frost is little more than an idea.
A napkin for your knees.

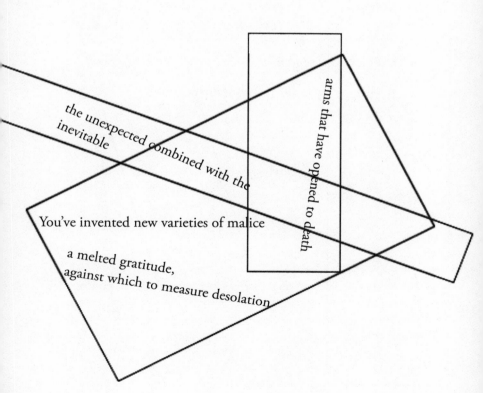

with no shelter in memory

the unexpected combined with the
inevitable

arms that have opened to death

You've invented new varieties of malice

a melted gratitude,
against which to measure desolation

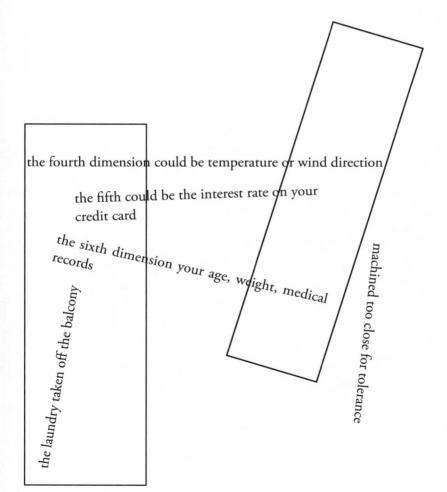

the fourth dimension could be temperature or wind direction

the fifth could be the interest rate on your
credit card

the sixth dimension your age, weight, medical
records

the laundry taken off the balcony

machined too close for tolerance

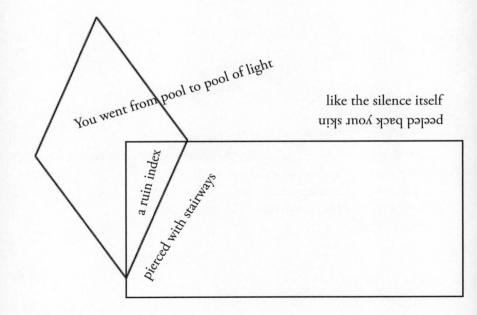

You went from pool to pool of light

like the silence itself
peeled back your skin

a ruin index

pierced with stairways

After dark, on these streets, under the ancient warehouse canopies, you.
Maledictions scratched into the steelwork.
The kindness of improvised spaces.
Your dense trembling, a dream of limbs, futureless,
unfractioned.

Cross between a dance and a fight.

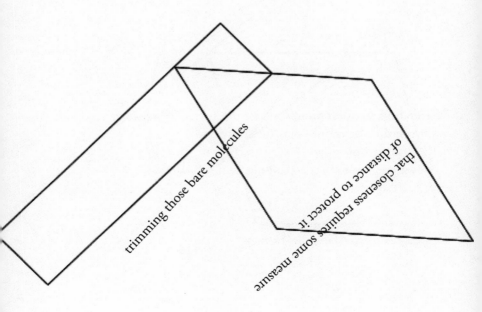

trimming those bare molecules

that closeness to protect it

of distance to protect it

some measure

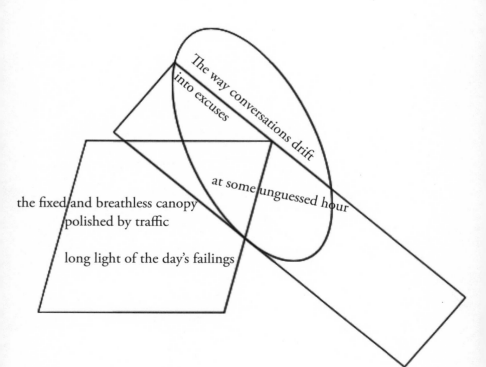

The way conversations drift
into excuses
at some unguessed hour
the fixed and breathless canopy
polished by traffic

long light of the day's failings

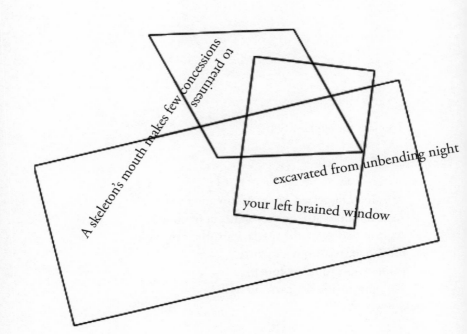

A skeleton's mouth makes few concessions to prettiness

to prettiness

excavated from unbending night

your left brained window

Too late for explanations.

At some unguessed hour. At any intensity.
As if to obliterate the very concept of clouds.
As if to seal away the predacious, the slow voice
of ruin, carved into a picture
frame you can never touch.
No light inside the cars, no light
anywhere.

Future Pastoral (Pripyat)

We are nothing but a bit of solar heat stored up and organized,
a reminder of the sun.

–Paul Cézanne

the light was surgical, binding

hoarsely caesium

As by palace
or pool

As it sponsor

turbined on barefoot

_____

There is no need to offer proof: some gestures are effective in real or imaginary worlds.

Born without genitals, born inside-out, armless, born without a mouth.

In this way furniture.

Like a world overexposed, a stage set.

Slightly lightly metallic tasting.

Whatever lack of air, wherever the chunks of graphite.

Twisted by their own breath.

instead of splinters, certainties

the same indifferent sun

last tide, broken, floating loose

this midnight on a corpus

in spite of

how everything happens

partial hinges, clamps

without witness

exactly like a statue

the breathing number

the disfigured sky

you can't interrupt

----

hand-laundry, the disfigured sky:

rest in sheer and locate

Or the depth of the grave, regardless

some dress-circle virtue

biting the hand till it bleeds

Or never walking

Or all that constitutes that deprivation

this strong, this healthy, this

Or those that don't know how to pray, and also pray

Or the coefficient

And out of deference no one dares smile

Or a very high number, impossibly out of scale

the long wash, the liquidating

Or signing the shovel

Our Slavic modesty coming through

Whatever the coefficient for the leakage

crawling, rolling, or sliding
outside of its skull

in this way furniture

and in this way cruel numbers

the ether that supported the wave

grapht fimbriate,   shoreless

weathered in wire

Ask any questions you will

dwarf torsos
                  in a jar,

elbow for an ear
or this frozen tumor, yes

            in serial light

It proved empty apart from
ourselves,
                  motionless

in this way ceramic, inevitable

devoid of reason

and in this way abandoned mid-lever

It was whole new stretches and it was the prospect of a world dropping away. More wolf than lion, more hyena

than either. Like a squint or a slight, the house itself a vegetal love.

because wedged between the weather and the obituaries

because sclerotic, baroque

                    because from the ground invisible, and because this
          crumpled
                blanket is a song

          because high corners & lush vegetation

          the salt fork

          floorboard seams

                    and because a museum of holes, because
                              the creeping dose

a kind of necklace

                              these pools too capable of remembering

because I envy the dogs and their shamelessness

Author's Note

A number of works were crucial to the writing of this book, either directly or indirectly, and I am no doubt greatly indebted to them. I wish to particularly acknowledge the following:

Somebody's Husband, Somebody's Son by Gordon Burn; *The Murder Room* by Michael Capuzzo — where I first learned of Albert Fish and his hideous letters; *Ratner's Star* by Don DeLillo; *Serial Killers* by Mark Seltzer; *Known and Strange Things* by Teju Cole; the paintings of Marita Hewitt; *The Recognitions* by William Gaddis; *Being Dead* by Jim Crace; *Stiff* by Mary Roach; *Natural Born Celebrities* by David Schmid; *Defiance* by Carole Maso; *Frost* by Thomas Bernhard; *Zero* by Ignacio de Loyola Brandão; *The Divine Sacrifice* by Tony Hays; *Requiem* by Curtis White; *True News* by Craig Watson; the music of Arvo Pärt; *Point and Line* by Thalia Field; *Child of God* and *Outer Dark* by Cormac McCarthy; *100 Suns* by Michael Light; the prints and paintings of William Scarlato; *Voices from Chernobyl* by Svetlana Alexievich; *Liar's Poker* by Michael Lewis; the paintings of Caravaggio; *Translating the Unspeakable* by Kathleen Fraser; David Simon's television show *The Wire*; *The King of Infinite Space* by Siobhan Roberts; *The Earth After Us* by Jan Zalesiewicz; and *Menahem Nahum of Chernobyl* translated by Arthur Green.

For the careful reading, diligence, well-timed sense of humor, and support, I'd like to thank my editors at Dalkey Archive Press: Nathan Redman, Jake Snyder, and John O'Brien.

For generous friendship and insightful conversations during the writing of this book, I'd like to especially thank Raymond Bianchi, Waltraud Haas, Dominick Mastrangelo, Martha Oatis, Sarah Ruhl, and Ilona Zineczko.

And for countless walks, conversations, Kalpitiya, navigating parental loss, weird sleep patterns, deserts and oceans, renovations, and for giving me the courage to believe in George Clooney, I'd like to thank my wife.

Mark Tardi is originally from Chicago and he earned his MFA from Brown University. His publications include the books *The Circus of Trust*, *Airport music*, and *Euclid Shudders*. A former Fulbright scholar, he lives with his wife and two dogs in a village in central Poland and is on the faculty at the University of Lodz.

MICHAL AJVAZ, *The Golden Age.*
The Other City.
PIERRE ALBERT-BIROT, *Grabinoulor.*
YUZ ALESHKOVSKY, *Kangaroo.*
FELIPE ALFAU, *Chromos.*
Locos.
JOE AMATO, *Samuel Taylor's Last Night.*
IVAN ÂNGELO, *The Celebration.*
The Tower of Glass.
ANTÓNIO LOBO ANTUNES, *Knowledge of Hell.*
The Splendor of Portugal.
ALAIN ARIAS-MISSON, *Theatre of Incest.*
JOHN ASHBERY & JAMES SCHUYLER, *A Nest of Ninnies.*
ROBERT ASHLEY, *Perfect Lives.*
GABRIELA AVIGUR-ROTEM, *Heatwave and Crazy Birds.*
DJUNA BARNES, *Ladies Almanack.*
Ryder.
JOHN BARTH, *Letters.*
Sabbatical.
DONALD BARTHELME, *The King.*
Paradise.
SVETISLAV BASARA, *Chinese Letter.*
MIQUEL BAUÇÀ, *The Siege in the Room.*
RENÉ BELLETTO, *Dying.*
MAREK BIENCZYK, *Transparency.*
ANDREI BITOV, *Pushkin House.*
ANDREJ BLATNIK, *You Do Understand.*
Law of Desire.
LOUIS PAUL BOON, *Chapel Road.*
My Little War.
Summer in Termuren.
ROGER BOYLAN, *Killoyle.*
IGNÁCIO DE LOYOLA BRANDÃO, *Anonymous Celebrity.*
Zero.
BONNIE BREMSER, *Troia: Mexican Memoirs.*
CHRISTINE BROOKE-ROSE, *Amalgamemnon.*
BRIGID BROPHY, *In Transit.*
The Prancing Novelist.

GERALD L. BRUNS, *Modern Poetry and the Idea of Language.*
GABRIELLE BURTON, *Heartbreak Hotel.*
MICHEL BUTOR, *Degrees.*
Mobile.
G. CABRERA INFANTE, *Infante's Inferno.*
Three Trapped Tigers.
JULIETA CAMPOS, *The Fear of Losing Eurydice.*
ANNE CARSON, *Eros the Bittersweet.*
ORLY CASTEL-BLOOM, *Dolly City.*
LOUIS-FERDINAND CÉLINE, *North.*
Conversations with Professor Y.
London Bridge.
MARIE CHAIX, *The Laurels of Lake Constance.*
HUGO CHARTERIS, *The Tide Is Right.*
ERIC CHEVILLARD, *Demolishing Nisard.*
The Author and Me.
MARC CHOLODENKO, *Mordechai Schamz.*
JOSHUA COHEN, *Witz.*
EMILY HOLMES COLEMAN, *The Shutter of Snow.*
ERIC CHEVILLARD, *The Author and Me.*
ROBERT COOVER, *A Night at the Movies.*
STANLEY CRAWFORD, *Log of the S.S. The Mrs Unguentine.*
Some Instructions to My Wife.
RENÉ CREVEL, *Putting My Foot in It.*
RALPH CUSACK, *Cadenza.*
NICHOLAS DELBANCO, *Sherbrookes.*
The Count of Concord.
NIGEL DENNIS, *Cards of Identity.*
PETER DIMOCK, *A Short Rhetoric for Leaving the Family.*
ARIEL DORFMAN, *Konfidenz.*
COLEMAN DOWELL, *Island People.*
Too Much Flesh and Jabez.
ARKADII DRAGOMOSHCHENKO, *Dust.*
RIKKI DUCORNET, *Phosphor in Dreamland.*
The Complete Butcher's Tales.

RIKKI DUCORNET (cont.), *The Jade Cabinet*.
The Fountains of Neptune.

WILLIAM EASTLAKE, *The Bamboo Bed*.
Castle Keep.
Lyric of the Circle Heart.

JEAN ECHENOZ, *Chopin's Move*.

STANLEY ELKIN, *A Bad Man*.
Criers and Kibitzers, Kibitzers and Criers.
The Dick Gibson Show.
The Franchiser.
The Living End.
Mrs. Ted Bliss.

FRANÇOIS EMMANUEL, *Invitation to a Voyage*.

PAUL EMOND, *The Dance of a Sham*.

SALVADOR ESPRIU, *Ariadne in the Grotesque Labyrinth*.

LESLIE A. FIEDLER, *Love and Death in the American Novel*.

JUAN FILLOY, *Op Oloop*.

ANDY FITCH, *Pop Poetics*.

GUSTAVE FLAUBERT, *Bouvard and Pécuchet*.

KASS FLEISHER, *Talking out of School*.

JON FOSSE, *Aliss at the Fire*.
Melancholy.

FORD MADOX FORD, *The March of Literature*.

MAX FRISCH, *I'm Not Stiller*.
Man in the Holocene.

CARLOS FUENTES, *Christopher Unborn*.
Distant Relations.
Terra Nostra.
Where the Air Is Clear.

TAKEHIKO FUKUNAGA, *Flowers of Grass*.

WILLIAM GADDIS, JR., *The Recognitions*.

JANICE GALLOWAY, *Foreign Parts*.
The Trick Is to Keep Breathing.

WILLIAM H. GASS, *Life Sentences*.
The Tunnel.
The World Within the Word.
Willie Masters' Lonesome Wife.

GÉRARD GAVARRY, *Hoppla! 1 2 3*.

ETIENNE GILSON, *The Arts of the Beautiful*.
Forms and Substances in the Arts.

C. S. GISCOMBE, *Giscome Road*.
Here.

DOUGLAS GLOVER, *Bad News of the Heart*.

WITOLD GOMBROWICZ, *A Kind of Testament*.

PAULO EMÍLIO SALES GOMES, *P's Three Women*.

GEORGI GOSPODINOV, *Natural Novel*.

JUAN GOYTISOLO, *Count Julian*.
Juan the Landless.
Makbara.
Marks of Identity.

HENRY GREEN, *Blindness*.
Concluding.
Doting.
Nothing.

JACK GREEN, *Fire the Bastards!*

JIŘÍ GRUŠA, *The Questionnaire*.

MELA HARTWIG, *Am I a Redundant Human Being?*

JOHN HAWKES, *The Passion Artist*.
Whistlejacket.

ELIZABETH HEIGHWAY, ED., *Contemporary Georgian Fiction*.

AIDAN HIGGINS, *Balcony of Europe*.
Blind Man's Bluff.
Bornholm Night-Ferry.
Langrishe, Go Down.
Scenes from a Receding Past.

KEIZO HINO, *Isle of Dreams*.

KAZUSHI HOSAKA, *Plainsong*.

ALDOUS HUXLEY, *Antic Hay*.
Point Counter Point.
Those Barren Leaves.
Time Must Have a Stop.

NAOYUKI II, *The Shadow of a Blue Cat*.

DRAGO JANČAR, *The Tree with No Name*.

MIKHEIL JAVAKHISHVILI, *Kvachi*.

GERT JONKE, *The Distant Sound*.
Homage to Czerny.
The System of Vienna.

JACQUES JOUET, *Mountain R.*
Savage.
Upstaged.
MIEKO KANAI, *The Word Book.*
YORAM KANIUK, *Life on Sandpaper.*
ZURAB KARUMIDZE, *Dagny.*
JOHN KELLY, *From Out of the City.*
HUGH KENNER, *Flaubert, Joyce and Beckett: The Stoic Comedians.*
Joyce's Voices.
DANILO KIŠ, *The Attic.*
The Lute and the Scars.
Psalm 44.
A Tomb for Boris Davidovich.
ANITA KONKKA, *A Fool's Paradise.*
GEORGE KONRÁD, *The City Builder.*
TADEUSZ KONWICKI, *A Minor Apocalypse.*
The Polish Complex.
ANNA KORDZAIA-SAMADASHVILI, *Me, Margarita.*
MENIS KOUMANDAREAS, *Koula.*
ELAINE KRAF, *The Princess of 72nd Street.*
JIM KRUSOE, *Iceland.*
AYSE KULIN, *Farewell: A Mansion in Occupied Istanbul.*
EMILIO LASCANO TEGUI, *On Elegance While Sleeping.*
ERIC LAURRENT, *Do Not Touch.*
VIOLETTE LEDUC, *La Bâtarde.*
EDOUARD LEVÉ, *Autoportrait.*
Newspaper.
Suicide.
Works.
MARIO LEVI, *Istanbul Was a Fairy Tale.*
DEBORAH LEVY, *Billy and Girl.*
JOSÉ LEZAMA LIMA, *Paradiso.*
ROSA LIKSOM, *Dark Paradise.*
OSMAN LINS, *Avalovara.*
The Queen of the Prisons of Greece.
FLORIAN LIPUŠ, *The Errors of Young Tjaž.*
GORDON LISH, *Peru.*
ALF MACLOCHLAINN, *Out of Focus.*
Past Habitual.

The Corpus in the Library.
RON LOEWINSOHN, *Magnetic Field(s).*
YURI LOTMAN, *Non-Memoirs.*
D. KEITH MANO, *Take Five.*
MINA LOY, *Stories and Essays of Mina Loy.*
MICHELINE AHARONIAN MARCOM, *A Brief History of Yes.*
The Mirror in the Well.
BEN MARCUS, *The Age of Wire and String.*
WALLACE MARKFIELD, *Teitlebaum's Window.*
DAVID MARKSON, *Reader's Block.*
Wittgenstein's Mistress.
CAROLE MASO, *AVA.*
HISAKI MATSUURA, *Triangle.*
LADISLAV MATEJKA & KRYSTYNA POMORSKA, EDS., *Readings in Russian Poetics: Formalist & Structuralist Views.*
HARRY MATHEWS, *Cigarettes.*
The Conversions.
The Human Country.
The Journalist.
My Life in CIA.
Singular Pleasures.
The Sinking of the Odradek.
Stadium.
Tlooth.
HISAKI MATSUURA, *Triangle.*
DONAL MCLAUGHLIN, *beheading the virgin mary, and other stories.*
JOSEPH MCELROY, *Night Soul and Other Stories.*
ABDELWAHAB MEDDEB, *Talismano.*
GERHARD MEIER, *Isle of the Dead.*
HERMAN MELVILLE, *The Confidence-Man.*
AMANDA MICHALOPOULOU, *I'd Like.*
STEVEN MILLHAUSER, *The Barnum Museum.*
In the Penny Arcade.
RALPH J. MILLS, JR., *Essays on Poetry.*
MOMUS, *The Book of Jokes.*
CHRISTINE MONTALBETTI, *The Origin of Man.*
Western.

NICHOLAS MOSLEY, *Accident.*
Assassins.
Catastrophe Practice.
A Garden of Trees.
Hopeful Monsters.
Imago Bird.
Inventing God.
Look at the Dark.
Metamorphosis.
Natalie Natalia.
Serpent.

WARREN MOTTE, *Fables of the Novel: French Fiction since 1990.*
Fiction Now: The French Novel in the 21st Century.
Mirror Gazing.
Oulipo: A Primer of Potential Literature.

GERALD MURNANE, *Barley Patch.*
Inland.

YVES NAVARRE, *Our Share of Time.*
Sweet Tooth.

DOROTHY NELSON, *In Night's City.*
Tar and Feathers.

ESHKOL NEVO, *Homesick.*

WILFRIDO D. NOLLEDO, *But for the Lovers.*

BORIS A. NOVAK, *The Master of Insomnia.*

FLANN O'BRIEN, *At Swim-Two-Birds.*
The Best of Myles.
The Dalkey Archive.
The Hard Life.
The Poor Mouth.
The Third Policeman.

CLAUDE OLLIER, *The Mise-en-Scène.*
Wert and the Life Without End.

PATRIK OUŘEDNÍK, *Europeana.*
The Opportune Moment, 1855.

BORIS PAHOR, *Necropolis.*

FERNANDO DEL PASO, *News from the Empire.*
Palinuro of Mexico.

ROBERT PINGET, *The Inquisitory.*
Mahu or The Material.
Trio.

MANUEL PUIG, *Betrayed by Rita Hayworth.*

The Buenos Aires Affair.
Heartbreak Tango.

RAYMOND QUENEAU, *The Last Days.*
Odile.
Pierrot Mon Ami.
Saint Glinglin.

ANN QUIN, *Berg.*
Passages.
Three.
Tripticks.

ISHMAEL REED, *The Free-Lance Pallbearers.*
The Last Days of Louisiana Red.
Ishmael Reed: The Plays.
Juice!
The Terrible Threes.
The Terrible Twos.
Yellow Back Radio Broke-Down.

JASIA REICHARDT, *15 Journeys Warsaw to London.*

JOÃO UBALDO RIBEIRO, *House of the Fortunate Buddhas.*

JEAN RICARDOU, *Place Names.*

RAINER MARIA RILKE,
The Notebooks of Malte Laurids Brigge.

JULIÁN RÍOS, *The House of Ulysses.*
Larva: A Midsummer Night's Babel.
Poundemonium.

ALAIN ROBBE-GRILLET, *Project for a Revolution in New York.*
A Sentimental Novel.

AUGUSTO ROA BASTOS, *I the Supreme.*

DANIËL ROBBERECHTS, *Arriving in Avignon.*

JEAN ROLIN, *The Explosion of the Radiator Hose.*

OLIVIER ROLIN, *Hotel Crystal.*

ALIX CLEO ROUBAUD, *Alix's Journal.*

JACQUES ROUBAUD, *The Form of a City Changes Faster, Alas, Than the Human Heart.*
The Great Fire of London.
Hortense in Exile.
Hortense Is Abducted.
Mathematics: The Plurality of Worlds of Lewis.
Some Thing Black.

RAYMOND ROUSSEL, *Impressions of Africa.*

VEDRANA RUDAN, *Night.*

PABLO M. RUIZ, *Four Cold Chapters on the Possibility of Literature.*

GERMAN SADULAEV, *The Maya Pill.*

TOMAŽ ŠALAMUN, *Soy Realidad.*

LYDIE SALVAYRE, *The Company of Ghosts.*
The Lecture.
The Power of Flies.

LUIS RAFAEL SÁNCHEZ, *Macho Camacho's Beat.*

SEVERO SARDUY, *Cobra & Maitreya.*

NATHALIE SARRAUTE, *Do You Hear Them?*
Martereau.
The Planetarium.

STIG SÆTERBAKKEN, *Siamese.*
Self-Control.
Through the Night.

ARNO SCHMIDT, *Collected Novellas.*
Collected Stories.
Nobodaddy's Children.
Two Novels.

ASAF SCHURR, *Motti.*

GAIL SCOTT, *My Paris.*

DAMION SEARLS, *What We Were Doing and Where We Were Going.*

JUNE AKERS SEESE, *Is This What Other Women Feel Too?*

BERNARD SHARE, *Inish.*
Transit.

VIKTOR SHKLOVSKY, *Bowstring.*
Literature and Cinematography.
Theory of Prose.
Third Factory.
Zoo, or Letters Not about Love.

PIERRE SINIAC, *The Collaborators.*

KJERSTI A. SKOMSVOLD, *The Faster I Walk, the Smaller I Am.*

JOSEF ŠKVORECKÝ, *The Engineer of Human Souls.*

GILBERT SORRENTINO, *Aberration of Starlight.*
Blue Pastoral.
Crystal Vision.

Imaginative Qualities of Actual Things.
Mulligan Stew. Red the Fiend.
Steelwork.
Under the Shadow.

MARKO SOSIČ, *Ballerina, Ballerina.*

ANDRZEJ STASIUK, *Dukla.*
Fado.

GERTRUDE STEIN, *The Making of Americans.*
A Novel of Thank You.

LARS SVENDSEN, *A Philosophy of Evil.*

PIOTR SZEWC, *Annihilation.*

GONÇALO M. TAVARES, *A Man: Klaus Klump.*
Jerusalem.
Learning to Pray in the Age of Technique.

LUCIAN DAN TEODOROVICI, *Our Circus Presents...*

NIKANOR TERATOLOGEN, *Assisted Living.*

STEFAN THEMERSON, *Hobson's Island.*
The Mystery of the Sardine.
Tom Harris.

TAEKO TOMIOKA, *Building Waves.*

JOHN TOOMEY, *Sleepwalker.*

DUMITRU TSEPENEAG, *Hotel Europa.*
The Necessary Marriage.
Pigeon Post.
Vain Art of the Fugue.

ESTHER TUSQUETS, *Stranded.*

DUBRAVKA UGRESIC, *Lend Me Your Character.*
Thank You for Not Reading.

TOR ULVEN, *Replacement.*

MATI UNT, *Brecht at Night.*
Diary of a Blood Donor.
Things in the Night.

ÁLVARO URIBE & OLIVIA SEARS, EDS., *Best of Contemporary Mexican Fiction.*

ELOY URROZ, *Friction.*
The Obstacles.

LUISA VALENZUELA, *Dark Desires and the Others.*
He Who Searches.

PAUL VERHAEGHEN, *Omega Minor.*

BORIS VIAN, *Heartsnatcher.*

LLORENÇ VILLALONGA, *The Dolls' Room*.

TOOMAS VINT, *An Unending Landscape*.

ORNELA VORPSI, *The Country Where No One Ever Dies*.

AUSTRYN WAINHOUSE, *Hedyphagetica*.

CURTIS WHITE, *America's Magic Mountain*.
The Idea of Home.
Memories of My Father Watching TV.
Requiem.

DIANE WILLIAMS,
Excitability: Selected Stories.
Romancer Erector.

DOUGLAS WOOLF, *Wall to Wall*.
Ya! & John-Juan.

JAY WRIGHT, *Polynomials and Pollen*.
The Presentable Art of Reading Absence.

PHILIP WYLIE, *Generation of Vipers*.

MARGUERITE YOUNG, *Angel in the Forest*.
Miss MacIntosh, My Darling.

REYOUNG, *Unbabbling*.

VLADO ŽABOT, *The Succubus*.

ZORAN ŽIVKOVIĆ , *Hidden Camera*.

LOUIS ZUKOFSKY, *Collected Fiction*.

VITOMIL ZUPAN, *Minuet for Guitar*.

SCOTT ZWIREN, *God Head*.

AND MORE . . .